SIBLEY

the Birder's Year

Baltimore Oriole
Icterus galbula

Written and illustrated by

David Allen Sibley

2010 WEEKLY ENGAGEMENT PLANNER

Published by Sellers Publishing, Inc., South Portland, Maine

Calendar © 2009 Sellers Publishing, Inc.
Text © 2000 David Sibley
Illustrations © 2000, 2002, 2003, 2009 David Sibley
All rights reserved.

Jewish holidays begin at sunset on the previous evening. Astronomical information is in Eastern Standard Time.
Key to abbreviations: United States (US), Canada (Can.), United Kingdom (UK), Australia (Austrl.),
New Zealand (NZ), New South Wales (NSW)

This calendar may not be reproduced by any means, including photocopying, without the prior written permission of the publisher.

SIBLEY
the Birder's Year

WINTER

Shows the normal winter distribution of the species. Many species are somewhat nomadic in winter, occupying only parts of the mapped range at any given time.

SUMMER

For virtually all species this is the breeding range and is more consistently and uniformly occupied than the winter range.

YEAR-ROUND

Indicates that the species can be found all year in this area, even though winter and summer populations may involve different individual birds. Only a few species are truly resident.

MIGRATION

Main migration routes are shown, as well as areas of regular dispersal and post-breeding wandering. Note that migration also passes through the summer and winter ranges.

RARE

Shows locations of rare occurrence (may be a single record or up to a few records a year).

KEY TO THE RANGE MAPS

PARTS OF A BIRD

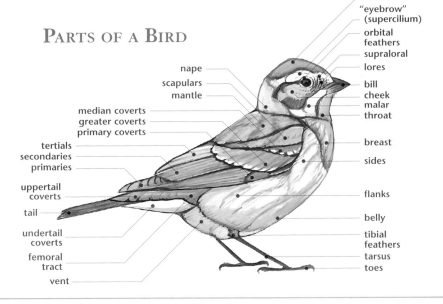

2010

JANUARY

S	M	T	W	T	F	S
					1	2
3	4	5	6	7	8	9
10	11	12	13	14	15	16
17	18	19	20	21	22	23
24	25	26	27	28	29	30
31						

FEBRUARY

S	M	T	W	T	F	S
	1	2	3	4	5	6
7	8	9	10	11	12	13
14	15	16	17	18	19	20
21	22	23	24	25	26	27
28						

MARCH

S	M	T	W	T	F	S
	1	2	3	4	5	6
7	8	9	10	11	12	13
14	15	16	17	18	19	20
21	22	23	24	25	26	27
28	29	30	31			

APRIL

S	M	T	W	T	F	S
				1	2	3
4	5	6	7	8	9	10
11	12	13	14	15	16	17
18	19	20	21	22	23	24
25	26	27	28	29	30	

MAY

S	M	T	W	T	F	S
						1
2	3	4	5	6	7	8
9	10	11	12	13	14	15
16	17	18	19	20	21	22
23	24	25	26	27	28	29
30	31					

JUNE

S	M	T	W	T	F	S
		1	2	3	4	5
6	7	8	9	10	11	12
13	14	15	16	17	18	19
20	21	22	23	24	25	26
27	28	29	30			

JULY

S	M	T	W	T	F	S
				1	2	3
4	5	6	7	8	9	10
11	12	13	14	15	16	17
18	19	20	21	22	23	24
25	26	27	28	29	30	31

AUGUST

S	M	T	W	T	F	S
1	2	3	4	5	6	7
8	9	10	11	12	13	14
15	16	17	18	19	20	21
22	23	24	25	26	27	28
29	30	31				

SEPTEMBER

S	M	T	W	T	F	S
			1	2	3	4
5	6	7	8	9	10	11
12	13	14	15	16	17	18
19	20	21	22	23	24	25
26	27	28	29	30		

OCTOBER

S	M	T	W	T	F	S
					1	2
3	4	5	6	7	8	9
10	11	12	13	14	15	16
17	18	19	20	21	22	23
24	25	26	27	28	29	30
31						

NOVEMBER

S	M	T	W	T	F	S
	1	2	3	4	5	6
7	8	9	10	11	12	13
14	15	16	17	18	19	20
21	22	23	24	25	26	27
28	29	30				

DECEMBER

S	M	T	W	T	F	S
			1	2	3	4
5	6	7	8	9	10	11
12	13	14	15	16	17	18
19	20	21	22	23	24	25
26	27	28	29	30	31	

January 2010

MONTH OVERVIEW

DECEMBER 2009
S M T W T F S
1 2 3 4 5
6 7 8 9 10 11 12
13 14 15 16 17 18 19
20 21 22 23 24 25 26
27 28 29 30 31

FEBRUARY
S M T W T F S
1 2 3 4 5 6
7 8 9 10 11 12 13
14 15 16 17 18 19 20
21 22 23 24 25 26 27
28

SUNDAY	MONDAY	TUESDAY	WEDNESDAY	THURSDAY	FRIDAY	SATURDAY
27	28	29	30	31	1 New Year's Day	2
3	4	5	6	7	8	9
10	11	12	13	14	15 Martin Luther King Jr.'s Birthday ● NEW MOON	16
17	18 Martin Luther King Jr.'s Birthday (observed)	19	20	21	22	23
24/31	25	26 Australia Day	27	28	29	30 ○ FULL MOON

Notes

Adult breeding

Adult breeding
(Mar–Oct)

Yellow-billed Loon
Gavia adamsii

Relatively thick-necked and long-billed;
bill angled up; appears small-eyed.
Peak of back at mid-body.

Length 35"
Wingspan 49"
Weight 11.8 lb (5,400 g)
    male > female

Key to Range Maps

WINTER
SUMMER
YEAR-ROUND
MIGRATION
RARE

December 2009/
January 2010

DECEMBER 2009

S	M	T	W	T	F	S
		1	2	3	4	5
6	7	8	9	10	11	12
13	14	15	16	17	18	19
20	21	22	23	24	25	26
27	28	29	30	31		

28 MONDAY

29 TUESDAY

FEBRUARY

S	M	T	W	T	F	S
	1	2	3	4	5	6
7	8	9	10	11	12	13
14	15	16	17	18	19	20
21	22	23	24	25	26	27
28						

30 WEDNESDAY

Notes

31 THURSDAY

New Year's Day

1 FRIDAY

Drizzle —
Mushrooming

2 SATURDAY

Mushrooming again
- lots coming up. Dinner w' Joy.

3 SUNDAY

Sunny - rode Duke
cleaning mushrooms.

WEEK 1

Adult

Adult breeding
(Feb-Sep)

Western Grebe
Aechmophorus occidentalis

Large and very slender with long neck
and long, thin bill. Clean dark gray
and white plumage.

Length 25"
Wingspan 24"
Weight 3.3 lb (1,500 g)

Key to Range Maps

WINTER
SUMMER
YEAR-ROUND
MIGRATION
RARE

January

DECEMBER 2009

S	M	T	W	T	F	S
		1	2	3	4	5
6	7	8	9	10	11	12
13	14	15	16	17	18	19
20	21	22	23	24	25	26
27	28	29	30	31		

FEBRUARY

S	M	T	W	T	F	S
	1	2	3	4	5	6
7	8	9	10	11	12	13
14	15	16	17	18	19	20
21	22	23	24	25	26	27
28						

4 MONDAY

5 TUESDAY

6 WEDNESDAY

Movies with Jackie

7 THURSDAY

Pen's Birthday.

8 FRIDAY

Sore Eye

9 SATURDAY

Went to Kaiser
Bailed Jesse out of Jail!

10 SUNDAY

mushrooming w' Jess
5 Crickets

Notes

WEEK 2

Darker adult

Darker adult

Manx Shearwater
Puffinus puffinus

Small, with dark auriculars with pale
crescent behind, white undertail coverts.

Length 13.5"
Wingspan 33"
Weight 1 lb (450 g)

Key to Range Maps

WINTER
SUMMER
YEAR-ROUND
MIGRATION
RARE

January

DECEMBER 2009
S	M	T	W	T	F	S
		1	2	3	4	5
6	7	8	9	10	11	12
13	14	15	16	17	18	19
20	21	22	23	24	25	26
27	28	29	30	31		

FEBRUARY
S	M	T	W	T	F	S
	1	2	3	4	5	6
7	8	9	10	11	12	13
14	15	16	17	18	19	20
21	22	23	24	25	26	27
28						

11 MONDAY

Gary's B'day

12 TUESDAY

Connie back from Mexico

13 WEDNESDAY

Notes

14 THURSDAY

rode Duke

15 FRIDAY

Martin Luther
King Jr.'s Birthday
● NEW MOON

16 SATURDAY

*mushrooming
7 buckets*

17 SUNDAY

*cleaning mushrooms
all day — Rain*

WEEK 3

Adult

flight relatively steady with low, banking
turns; glides with wings bowed

Adult

Band-rumped Storm-Petrel
Oceanodroma castro

Scarce and prefers warm water. Note white on
undertail coverts, dark upperwing.

Length 9"
Wingspan 19"
Weight 1.5 oz (42 g)

Key to Range Maps

WINTER
SUMMER
YEAR-ROUND
MIGRATION
RARE

January

DECEMBER 2009

S	M	T	W	T	F	S
		1	2	3	4	5
6	7	8	9	10	11	12
13	14	15	16	17	18	19
20	21	22	23	24	25	26
27	28	29	30	31		

FEBRUARY

S	M	T	W	T	F	S
	1	2	3	4	5	6
7	8	9	10	11	12	13
14	15	16	17	18	19	20
21	22	23	24	25	26	27
28						

18 MONDAY — Martin Luther King Jr.'s Birthday (observed)

rain

19 TUESDAY

Jess brought me 6 bottles
rain
— storming premium
Chardonnay!

Notes

20 WEDNESDAY

Jess brought me
more rain. Olive Oil

21 THURSDAY

still raining !

22 FRIDAY

Dinner w' Annie

23 SATURDAY

Mushrooming
10 buckets !

24 SUNDAY

Cleaning mushrooms
all day

WEEK 4

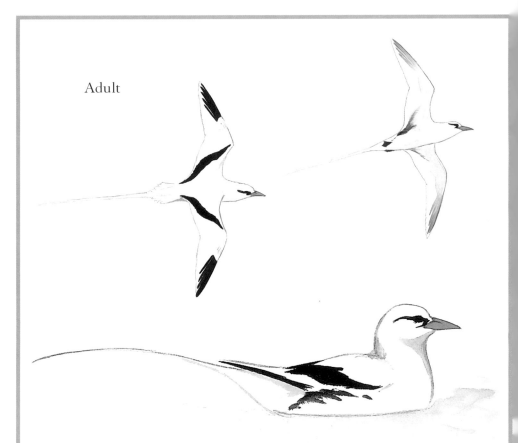

Adult

Adult

White-tailed Tropicbird
Phaethon lepturus

This species of oceanic bird is found in warm
water, often seen resting on the water.
Note short, dark eye-line.

Length 15" (adult to 29")
Wingspan 37"
Weight 11 oz (300 g)

Key to Range Maps

WINTER

SUMMER

YEAR-ROUND

MIGRATION

RARE

January

DECEMBER 2009

S	M	T	W	T	F	S
		1	2	3	4	5
6	7	8	9	10	11	12
13	14	15	16	17	18	19
20	21	22	23	24	25	26
27	28	29	30	31		

FEBRUARY

S	M	T	W	T	F	S
	1	2	3	4	5	6
7	8	9	10	11	12	13
14	15	16	17	18	19	20
21	22	23	24	25	26	27
28						

25 MONDAY

rain

Took mushrooms to Connie

26 TUESDAY   Australia Day

Murray 3.

27 WEDNESDAY

28 THURSDAY   *Dan's Birthday*

29 FRIDAY

30 SATURDAY   ○ FULL MOON

31 SUNDAY

Notes

February 2010

MONTH OVERVIEW

JANUARY
S	M	T	W	T	F	S
					1	2
3	4	5	6	7	8	9
10	11	12	13	14	15	16
17	18	19	20	21	22	23
24	25	26	27	28	29	30
31						

MARCH
S	M	T	W	T	F	S
	1	2	3	4	5	6
7	8	9	10	11	12	13
14	15	16	17	18	19	20
21	22	23	24	25	26	27
28	29	30	31			

SUNDAY	MONDAY	TUESDAY	WEDNESDAY	THURSDAY	FRIDAY	SATURDAY
31	1	2 Groundhog Day	3	4	5	6 Waitangi Day (New Zealand)
7	8	9	10	11	12 Lincoln's Birthday	13 ● New Moon
14 Valentine's Day Chinese New Year	15 Presidents' Day (observed)	16	17 Ash Wednesday	18	19	20
21	22 Washington's Birthday	23	24	25	26	27
28 ○ Full Moon	1	2	3	4	5	6

Notes

Adult

Adult breeding
(Feb-Jul)

Snowy Egret
Egretta thula

Small and slender; yellow feet contrasting
with dark legs distinctive. Always white,
often gather in loose flocks and feed
mainly on fish captured in open water.

Length 24"
Wingspan 41"
Weight 13 oz (360 g)

Key to Range Maps

WINTER
SUMMER
YEAR-ROUND
MIGRATION
RARE

February

		JANUARY				
S	M	T	W	T	F	S
					1	2
3	4	5	6	7	8	9
10	11	12	13	14	15	16
17	18	19	20	21	22	23
24	25	26	27	28	29	30
31						

		MARCH				
S	M	T	W	T	F	S
	1	2	3	4	5	6
7	8	9	10	11	12	13
14	15	16	17	18	19	20
21	22	23	24	25	26	27
28	29	30	31			

1 | MONDAY

2 | TUESDAY — Groundhog Day

3 | WEDNESDAY

4 | THURSDAY

5 | FRIDAY

6 | SATURDAY — Waitangi Day (New Zealand)

7 | SUNDAY

Notes

WEEK 6

Adult

Adult breeding
(Feb-Jul)

Juvenile
(Jul-Feb)

Tricolored Heron
Egretta tricolor

Extremely long-necked and long-billed;
very active. Note bicolored underparts.
Usually solitary, they catch fish in
shallow water.

Length 26"
Wingspan 36"
Weight 13 oz (380 g)

Key to Range Maps

WINTER
SUMMER
YEAR-ROUND
MIGRATION
RARE

February

JANUARY
S	M	T	W	T	F	S
					1	2
3	4	5	6	7	8	9
10	11	12	13	14	15	16
17	18	19	20	21	22	23
24	25	26	27	28	29	30
31						

MARCH
S	M	T	W	T	F	S
	1	2	3	4	5	6
7	8	9	10	11	12	13
14	15	16	17	18	19	20
21	22	23	24	25	26	27
28	29	30	31			

8 MONDAY

9 TUESDAY

10 WEDNESDAY

11 THURSDAY

12 FRIDAY

Lincoln's Birthday

13 SATURDAY

● NEW MOON

14 SUNDAY

Valentine's Day
Chinese New Year

Notes

Adult male

Adult male breeding
(Oct-Jun)

Ring-necked Duck
Aythya collaris

Compact; distinctive peaked head, dark
back, pale "spur" on breast sides. Rises
easily from water; flight more erratic and
twisting than other Aythya ducks.

Length 17"
Wingspan 25"
Weight 1.5 lb (700 g)
   male > female

Key to Range Maps

WINTER
SUMMER
YEAR-ROUND
MIGRATION
RARE

February

JANUARY						
S	M	T	W	T	F	S
				1	2
3	4	5	6	7	8	9
10	11	12	13	14	15	16
17	18	19	20	21	22	23
24	25	26	27	28	29	30
31						

MARCH						
S	M	T	W	T	F	S
	1	2	3	4	5	6
7	8	9	10	11	12	13
14	15	16	17	18	19	20
21	22	23	24	25	26	27
28	29	30	31			

15 | MONDAY   Presidents' Day (observed)

16 | TUESDAY

17 | WEDNESDAY   Ash Wednesday

18 | THURSDAY

19 | FRIDAY

20 | SATURDAY

21 | SUNDAY

Notes

WEEK 8

Adult male spring

Male landing

Adult female spring
(May-Jun)

flight rapid, rising and
falling, twisting, low over water;
wingbeats below horizontal

Long-tailed Duck
Clangula hyemalis

Round body; short, pointed, dark wings
distinctive in all plumages. Formerly
known as Oldsquaw.

Length 16.5"
  (adult male to 21")
Wingspan 28"
Weight 1.6 lb (740 g)
  male > female

Key to Range Maps

WINTER
SUMMER
YEAR-ROUND
MIGRATION
RARE

February

JANUARY

S	M	T	W	T	F	S
				1	2	
3	4	5	6	7	8	9
10	11	12	13	14	15	16
17	18	19	20	21	22	23
24	25	26	27	28	29	30
31						

MARCH

S	M	T	W	T	F	S
	1	2	3	4	5	6
7	8	9	10	11	12	13
14	15	16	17	18	19	20
21	22	23	24	25	26	27
28	29	30	31			

22 | MONDAY   Washington's Birthday

23 | TUESDAY

24 | WEDNESDAY   Mum's Birthday

25 | THURSDAY

26 | FRIDAY

27 | SATURDAY

28 | SUNDAY   ◯ FULL MOON

Notes

WEEK 9

March 2010

MONTH OVERVIEW

FEBRUARY

S	M	T	W	T	F	S
	1	2	3	4	5	6
7	8	9	10	11	12	13
14	15	16	17	18	19	20
21	22	23	24	25	26	27
28						

APRIL

S	M	T	W	T	F	S
				1	2	3
4	5	6	7	8	9	10
11	12	13	14	15	16	17
18	19	20	21	22	23	24
25	26	27	28	29	30	

SUNDAY	MONDAY	TUESDAY	WEDNESDAY	THURSDAY	FRIDAY	SATURDAY
28	1 Labour Day (W. Australia)	2	3	4	5	6
7	8 International Women's Day Labour Day (Victoria) Commonwealth Day (UK) Canberra Day (Australia)	9	10	11	12	13
14 Daylight Saving begins	15 ● NEW MOON	16	17 St. Patrick's Day	18	19	20 Vernal Equinox
21	22	23	24	25	26	27
28 Palm Sunday	29 ○ FULL MOON	30 Passover begins	31	1	2	3

Notes

gliding

wingbeats deep, loose

soaring

Adult male

Adult

Mississippi Kite

Ictinia mississippiensis

Falconlike shape but more buoyant flight; wings broadest at wrist; short outermost primary distinctive.

Length 14"
Wingspan 31"
Weight 10 oz (280 g)

Key to Range Maps

WINTER
SUMMER
YEAR-ROUND
MIGRATION
RARE

March

FEBRUARY

S	M	T	W	T	F	S
	1	2	3	4	5	6
7	8	9	10	11	12	13
14	15	16	17	18	19	20
21	22	23	24	25	26	27
28						

APRIL

S	M	T	W	T	F	S
				1	2	3
4	5	6	7	8	9	10
11	12	13	14	15	16	17
18	19	20	21	22	23	24
25	26	27	28	29	30	

1 MONDAY   Labour Day (W. Australia)

2 TUESDAY

3 WEDNESDAY

4 THURSDAY

5 FRIDAY

6 SATURDAY

7 SUNDAY

Notes

WEEK 10

Adult male

Adult

Northern Goshawk
Accipiter gentilis

Large, relatively stocky with broad body;
short, broad tail; long, fairly pointed
wings.

Length 21"
Wingspan 41"
Weight 2.1 lb (950 g)
female > male

Key to Range Maps

WINTER
SUMMER
YEAR-ROUND
MIGRATION
RARE

March

FEBRUARY

S	M	T	W	T	F	S
	1	2	3	4	5	6
7	8	9	10	11	12	13
14	15	16	17	18	19	20
21	22	23	24	25	26	27
28						

APRIL

S	M	T	W	T	F	S
				1	2	3
4	5	6	7	8	9	10
11	12	13	14	15	16	17
18	19	20	21	22	23	24
25	26	27	28	29	30	

8 | MONDAY

International Women's Day
Labour Day (Victoria)
Commonwealth Day (UK)
Canberra Day (Australia)

9 | TUESDAY

10 | WEDNESDAY

11 | THURSDAY

12 | FRIDAY

13 | SATURDAY

14 | SUNDAY

Daylight Saving begins

Notes

Intermediate adult

Intermediate juvenile (1st year)

Intermediate adult

Swainson's Hawk
Buteo swainsoni

Our most slender buteo; relatively long tail, long and fairly pointed wings; note dark remiges.

Length 19"
Wingspan 51"
Weight 1.9 lb (855 g)
 female > male

Key to Range Maps

WINTER
SUMMER
YEAR-ROUND
MIGRATION
RARE

March

FEBRUARY

S	M	T	W	T	F	S
	1	2	3	4	5	6
7	8	9	10	11	12	13
14	15	16	17	18	19	20
21	22	23	24	25	26	27
28						

APRIL

S	M	T	W	T	F	S
				1	2	3
4	5	6	7	8	9	10
11	12	13	14	15	16	17
18	19	20	21	22	23	24
25	26	27	28	29	30	

15 | MONDAY   ● NEW MOON

16 | TUESDAY

17 | WEDNESDAY   St. Patrick's Day

18 | THURSDAY

19 | FRIDAY

20 | SATURDAY   Vernal Equinox

21 | SUNDAY

Notes

Adult

Adult

Osprey
Pandion haliaetus

Long, narrow wings always angled and bowed down; gull-like. Shape and underwing pattern distinctive.

Length 23"
Wingspan 63"
Weight 3.5 lb (1,600 g)

Key to Range Maps

WINTER

SUMMER

YEAR-ROUND

MIGRATION

RARE

March

FEBRUARY

S	M	T	W	T	F	S
	1	2	3	4	5	6
7	8	9	10	11	12	13
14	15	16	17	18	19	20
21	22	23	24	25	26	27
28						

APRIL

S	M	T	W	T	F	S
				1	2	3
4	5	6	7	8	9	10
11	12	13	14	15	16	17
18	19	20	21	22	23	24
25	26	27	28	29	30	

22 | MONDAY

23 | TUESDAY

Notes

24 | WEDNESDAY

25 | THURSDAY

26 | FRIDAY

27 | SATURDAY

28 | SUNDAY | Palm Sunday

April 2010

MONTH OVERVIEW

MARCH

S	M	T	W	T	F	S
	1	2	3	4	5	6
7	8	9	10	11	12	13
14	15	16	17	18	19	20
21	22	23	24	25	26	27
28	29	30	31			

MAY

S	M	T	W	T	F	S
						1
2	3	4	5	6	7	8
9	10	11	12	13	14	15
16	17	18	19	20	21	22
23	24	25	26	27	28	29
30	31					

SUNDAY	MONDAY	TUESDAY	WEDNESDAY	THURSDAY	FRIDAY	SATURDAY
28	29	30	31	1	2 Good Friday	3
4 Easter Sunday	5 Easter Monday (Can., UK, Austrl., NZ)	6	7	8	9	10
11 Holocaust Remembrance Day	12	13	14 ● NEW MOON	15	16	17
18	19	20	21	22 Earth Day	23	24
25 ANZAC Day (Austrl., NZ, NSW, Queensland)	26	27	28 ○ FULL MOON	29	30 Arbor Day	1

Notes

Adult male

Adult male

Adult female

American Kestrel
Falco sparverius

Our smallest and most delicate
falcon; long-winged and long-tailed.
Wingtips blunt when spread,
often swept back.

Length 9"
Wingspan 22"
Weight 4.1 oz (117 g)
   female > male

Key to Range Maps

WINTER
SUMMER
YEAR-ROUND
MIGRATION
RARE

March/April

MARCH						
S	M	T	W	T	F	S
	1	2	3	4	5	6
7	8	9	10	11	12	13
14	15	16	17	18	19	20
21	22	23	24	25	26	27
28	29	30	31			

29 | MONDAY ○ FULL MOON

MAY						
S	M	T	W	T	F	S
						1
2	3	4	5	6	7	8
9	10	11	12	13	14	15
16	17	18	19	20	21	22
23	24	25	26	27	28	29
30	31					

30 | TUESDAY Passover begins

Notes

31 | WEDNESDAY

1 | THURSDAY

2 | FRIDAY Good Friday

3 | SATURDAY

4 | SUNDAY Easter Sunday

WEEK 14

Adult female
breeding

Adult female
breeding
(May-Jul)

Rock Ptarmigan
Lagopus mutus

This species is found on barren, rocky
tundra; found singly in summer and in
small flocks in winter.

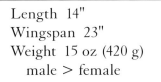

Length 14"
Wingspan 23"
Weight 15 oz (420 g)
    male > female

Key to Range Maps

WINTER
SUMMER
YEAR-ROUND
MIGRATION
RARE

April

MARCH
S	M	T	W	T	F	S
		1	2	3	4	5	6
7	8	9	10	11	12	13
14	15	16	17	18	19	20
21	22	23	24	25	26	27
28	29	30	31			

MAY
S	M	T	W	T	F	S
						1
2	3	4	5	6	7	8
9	10	11	12	13	14	15
16	17	18	19	20	21	22
23	24	25	26	27	28	29
30	31					

5 MONDAY

Easter Monday
(Can., UK, Austrl., NZ)

6 TUESDAY

7 WEDNESDAY

8 THURSDAY

9 FRIDAY

10 SATURDAY

11 SUNDAY

Holocaust
Remembrance Day

Notes

WEEK 15

Adult breeding

Adult male breeding
(Apr-Sep)

Black-bellied Plover
Pluvialis squatarola

Our largest plover, with relatively large
head and large, heavy bill; white tail
and black axillaries distinctive.

Length 11.5"
Wingspan 29"
Weight 8 oz (240 g)

Key to Range Maps

WINTER
SUMMER
YEAR-ROUND
MIGRATION
RARE

April

MARCH

S	M	T	W	T	F	S
		1	2	3	4	5	6
7	8	9	10	11	12	13
14	15	16	17	18	19	20
21	22	23	24	25	26	27
28	29	30	31			

MAY

S	M	T	W	T	F	S
						1
2	3	4	5	6	7	8
9	10	11	12	13	14	15
16	17	18	19	20	21	22
23	24	25	26	27	28	29
30	31					

12 | MONDAY

13 | TUESDAY

14 | WEDNESDAY ● NEW MOON

15 | THURSDAY

16 | FRIDAY

17 | SATURDAY

18 | SUNDAY

Notes

Adult American

Worn adult
(Apr–Oct)

Whimbrel
Numenius phaeopus

This primarily coastal species is found on
marshes, beaches, and rocky shores, often
in flocks, but it forages singly. American
population grayish-brown overall.

Length 17.5"
Wingspan 32"
Weight 14 oz (390 g)
    female > male

Key to Range Maps
WINTER
SUMMER
YEAR-ROUND
MIGRATION
RARE

April

MARCH

S	M	T	W	T	F	S
	1	2	3	4	5	6
7	8	9	10	11	12	13
14	15	16	17	18	19	20
21	22	23	24	25	26	27
28	29	30	31			

MAY

S	M	T	W	T	F	S
						1
2	3	4	5	6	7	8
9	10	11	12	13	14	15
16	17	18	19	20	21	22
23	24	25	26	27	28	29
30	31					

19 MONDAY

20 TUESDAY

21 WEDNESDAY

22 THURSDAY — Earth Day

23 FRIDAY

24 SATURDAY

25 SUNDAY — ANZAC Day
(Austrl., NZ, NSW, Queensland)

Notes

May 2010

MONTH OVERVIEW

APRIL

S	M	T	W	T	F	S
				1	2	3
4	5	6	7	8	9	10
11	12	13	14	15	16	17
18	19	20	21	22	23	24
25	26	27	28	29	30	

JUNE

S	M	T	W	T	F	S
		1	2	3	4	5
6	7	8	9	10	11	12
13	14	15	16	17	18	19
20	21	22	23	24	25	26
27	28	29	30			

SUNDAY	MONDAY	TUESDAY	WEDNESDAY	THURSDAY	FRIDAY	SATURDAY
25	26	27	28	29	30	1 May Day
2	3 Bank Holiday (UK) Labour Day (Queensland)	4	5	6	7	8
9 Mother's Day	10	11	12	13 ● New Moon	14	15 Armed Forces Day
16	17	18	19	20	21	22
23/30 Memorial Day (30th)	24/31 Victoria Day (24th) (Canada) Memorial Day (31st) (observed) Bank Holiday (31st) (UK)	25	26	27 ○ Full Moon	28	29

Notes

Adult breeding

Adult male breeding (Apr-Sep)

Adult female breeding (Apr-Sep)

Red Phalarope
Phalaropus fulicaria

Phalaropes nest on tundra ponds and winter in small flocks along weed lines on open ocean.

Length 8.5"
Wingspan 17"
Weight 1.9 oz (55 g)
    female > male

Key to Range Maps

WINTER
SUMMER
YEAR-ROUND
MIGRATION
RARE

April/May

APRIL

S	M	T	W	T	F	S
				1	2	3
4	5	6	7	8	9	10
11	12	13	14	15	16	17
18	19	20	21	22	23	24
25	26	27	28	29	30	

JUNE

S	M	T	W	T	F	S
		1	2	3	4	5
6	7	8	9	10	11	12
13	14	15	16	17	18	19
20	21	22	23	24	25	26
27	28	29	30			

26 | MONDAY

27 | TUESDAY

28 | WEDNESDAY   ○ FULL MOON

29 | THURSDAY

30 | FRIDAY   Arbor Day

1 | SATURDAY   May Day

2 | SUNDAY

Notes

WEEK 18

Adult

Juvenile
(Jun-Sep)

Adult breeding
(Jan-Sep)

Sooty Tern
Sterna fuscata

This species is found over warm water;
sooty virtually never perches
except at nest site.

Length 16"
Wingspan 32"
Weight 6 oz (180 g)

Key to Range Maps
WINTER
SUMMER
YEAR-ROUND
MIGRATION
RARE

May

APRIL

S	M	T	W	T	F	S
				1	2	3
4	5	6	7	8	9	10
11	12	13	14	15	16	17
18	19	20	21	22	23	24
25	26	27	28	29	30	

JUNE

S	M	T	W	T	F	S
	1	2	3	4	5	
6	7	8	9	10	11	12
13	14	15	16	17	18	19
20	21	22	23	24	25	26
27	28	29	30			

3 MONDAY — Bank Holiday (UK) / Labour Day (Queensland)

4 TUESDAY

5 WEDNESDAY

6 THURSDAY

7 FRIDAY

8 SATURDAY

9 SUNDAY — Mother's Day

Notes

Adult Eastern

wingbeats steady, stiff,
mostly below horizontal

Adult Eastern

Great
Horned Owl
Bubo virginianus

Large (like Red-tailed Hawk) and bulky,
with broad body and large head; stout
ear-tufts create catlike head shape.

Length 22"
Wingspan 44"
Weight 3.1 lb (1,400 g)
female > male

Key to Range Maps

WINTER
SUMMER
YEAR-ROUND
MIGRATION
RARE

May

APRIL

S	M	T	W	T	F	S
				1	2	3
4	5	6	7	8	9	10
11	12	13	14	15	16	17
18	19	20	21	22	23	24
25	26	27	28	29	30	

JUNE

S	M	T	W	T	F	S
		1	2	3	4	5
6	7	8	9	10	11	12
13	14	15	16	17	18	19
20	21	22	23	24	25	26
27	28	29	30			

10 | MONDAY

11 | TUESDAY

12 | WEDNESDAY

13 | THURSDAY ● NEW MOON

14 | FRIDAY

15 | SATURDAY — Armed Forces Day

16 | SUNDAY

Notes

WEEK 20

Adult

Adult

Adult

Fledging
(May-Sep)

Elf Owl
Micrathene whitneyi

Tiny — our smallest owl — and relatively small-headed. Finely speckled gray overall.

Length 5.75"
Wingspan 13"
Weight 1.4 oz (40 g)

Key to Range Maps

WINTER
SUMMER
YEAR-ROUND
MIGRATION
RARE

May

APRIL

S	M	T	W	T	F	S
				1	2	3
4	5	6	7	8	9	10
11	12	13	14	15	16	17
18	19	20	21	22	23	24
25	26	27	28	29	30	

JUNE

S	M	T	W	T	F	S
		1	2	3	4	5
6	7	8	9	10	11	12
13	14	15	16	17	18	19
20	21	22	23	24	25	26
27	28	29	30			

17 | MONDAY

18 | TUESDAY

19 | WEDNESDAY

20 | THURSDAY

21 | FRIDAY

22 | SATURDAY

23 | SUNDAY

Notes

Adult male

Adult male

Common Nighthawk
Chordeiles minor

Larger and longer-winged than other
nighthawks. Primaries project beyond
tail tip at rest. Most are white-bellied,
but some are as buffy as other night-
hawk species.

Length 9.5"
Wingspan 24"
Weight 2.2 oz (62 g)

Key to Range Maps

WINTER
SUMMER
YEAR-ROUND
MIGRATION
RARE

May

APRIL

S	M	T	W	T	F	S
				1	2	3
4	5	6	7	8	9	10
11	12	13	14	15	16	17
18	19	20	21	22	23	24
25	26	27	28	29	30	

JUNE

S	M	T	W	T	F	S
		1	2	3	4	5
6	7	8	9	10	11	12
13	14	15	16	17	18	19
20	21	22	23	24	25	26
27	28	29	30			

24 | MONDAY — Victoria Day (Canada)

25 | TUESDAY

26 | WEDNESDAY

27 | THURSDAY — ◯ FULL MOON

28 | FRIDAY

29 | SATURDAY

30 | SUNDAY — Memorial Day

Notes

WEEK 22

June 2010

MONTH OVERVIEW

MAY
S M T W T F S
                    1
2 3 4 5 6 7 8
9 10 11 12 13 14 15
16 17 18 19 20 21 22
23 24 25 26 27 28 29
30 31

JULY
S M T W T F S
            1 2 3
4 5 6 7 8 9 10
11 12 13 14 15 16 17
18 19 20 21 22 23 24
25 26 27 28 29 30 31

Sunday	Monday	Tuesday	Wednesday	Thursday	Friday	Saturday
30	31	1	2	3	4	5
6	7 Queen's Birthday (New Zealand)	8	9	10	11	12 ● New Moon
13	14 Flag Day Queen's Birthday (Australia)	15	16	17	18	19
20 Father's Day	21 Summer Solstice	22	23	24	25	26 ○ Full Moon
27	28	29	30	1	2	3

Notes

Juvenile female
(Feb-Sep)

red crown
and throat

Adult male

Adult male

Anna's Hummingbird
Calypte anna

Large and sturdy-looking; tubular
body with tail held stationary and
in line with body. Short, straight bill
and long, sloping forehead.

Length 4"
Wingspan 5.25"
Weight 0.15 oz (4.3g)

Key to Range Maps

WINTER
SUMMER
YEAR-ROUND
MIGRATION
RARE

May/June

MAY
S	M	T	W	T	F	S
						1
2	3	4	5	6	7	8
9	10	11	12	13	14	15
16	17	18	19	20	21	22
23	24	25	26	27	28	29
30	31					

JULY
S	M	T	W	T	F	S
				1	2	3
4	5	6	7	8	9	10
11	12	13	14	15	16	17
18	19	20	21	22	23	24
25	26	27	28	29	30	31

31 | MONDAY

Memorial Day
(observed)
Bank Holiday (UK)

1 | TUESDAY

2 | WEDNESDAY

3 | THURSDAY

4 | FRIDAY

5 | SATURDAY

6 | SUNDAY

Notes

WEEK 23

Adult male

Adult female

Adult male

Belted Kingfisher
Ceryle alcyon

Familiar and widespread. Like other
kingfishers; very large-headed with
long, heavy bill and short tail; legs
very short.

Length 13"
Wingspan 20"
Weight 5 oz (150 g)

Key to Range Maps

WINTER
SUMMER
YEAR-ROUND
MIGRATION
RARE

June

MAY

S	M	T	W	T	F	S
						1
2	3	4	5	6	7	8
9	10	11	12	13	14	15
16	17	18	19	20	21	22
23	24	25	26	27	28	29
30	31					

JULY

S	M	T	W	T	F	S
				1	2	3
4	5	6	7	8	9	10
11	12	13	14	15	16	17
18	19	20	21	22	23	24
25	26	27	28	29	30	31

7 | MONDAY   Queen's Birthday
                                       (New Zealand)

8 | TUESDAY

9 | WEDNESDAY

10 | THURSDAY

11 | FRIDAY

12 | SATURDAY   ● NEW MOON

13 | SUNDAY

Notes

Adult female Eastern

Adult female
Eastern

Hairy
Woodpecker
Picoides villosus

Large and strong, with relatively long
and sturdy bill. Favors more mature
woods and larger branches; it never
forages on weed stalks.

Length 9.25"
Wingspan 15"
Weight 2.3 oz (66 g)
   male > female

Key to Range Maps

WINTER

SUMMER

YEAR-ROUND

MIGRATION

RARE

June

MAY

S	M	T	W	T	F	S
						1
2	3	4	5	6	7	8
9	10	11	12	13	14	15
16	17	18	19	20	21	22
23	24	25	26	27	28	29
30	31					

JULY

S	M	T	W	T	F	S
				1	2	3
4	5	6	7	8	9	10
11	12	13	14	15	16	17
18	19	20	21	22	23	24
25	26	27	28	29	30	31

14 | MONDAY

Flag Day
Queen's Birthday
(Australia)

15 | TUESDAY

16 | WEDNESDAY

17 | THURSDAY

18 | FRIDAY

19 | SATURDAY

20 | SUNDAY

Father's Day

Notes

Adult

Adult

Great Crested Flycatcher
Myiarchus crinitus

Found mainly in hardwood forests.
Large and fairly heavy; with long
wings. Note brighter colors than
any other Myiarchus.

Length 8.75"
Wingspan 13"
Weight 1.2 oz (34 g)

Key to Range Maps

WINTER
SUMMER
YEAR-ROUND
MIGRATION
RARE

June

		MAY				
S	M	T	W	T	F	S
						1
2	3	4	5	6	7	8
9	10	11	12	13	14	15
16	17	18	19	20	21	22
23	24	25	26	27	28	29
30	31					

		JULY				
S	M	T	W	T	F	S
				1	2	3
4	5	6	7	8	9	10
11	12	13	14	15	16	17
18	19	20	21	22	23	24
25	26	27	28	29	30	31

21 MONDAY   Summer Solstice

22 TUESDAY

23 WEDNESDAY

24 THURSDAY

25 FRIDAY

26 SATURDAY   ○ FULL MOON

27 SUNDAY

Notes

July 2010

MONTH OVERVIEW

JUNE
S M T W T F S
1 2 3 4 5
6 7 8 9 10 11 12
13 14 15 16 17 18 19
20 21 22 23 24 25 26
27 28 29 30

AUGUST
S M T W T F S
1 2 3 4 5 6 7
8 9 10 11 12 13 14
15 16 17 18 19 20 21
22 23 24 25 26 27 28
29 30 31

SUNDAY	MONDAY	TUESDAY	WEDNESDAY	THURSDAY	FRIDAY	SATURDAY
27	28	29	30	1 Canada Day	2	3
4 Independence Day	5	6	7	8	9	10
11 ● NEW MOON	12	13	14	15	16	17
18	19	20	21	22	23	24
25 ○ FULL MOON	26	27	28	29	30	31

Notes

Adult

Lighter adult

Lighter adult

Loggerhead Shrike
Lanius ludovicianus

Large-headed with stout, conical bill;
Shrikes are found singly in open,
brushy fields, hedgerows, and
the edges of woods.

Length 9"
Wingspan 12"
Weight 1.7 oz (48 g)

Key to Range Maps

WINTER

SUMMER

YEAR-ROUND

MIGRATION

RARE

June/July

JUNE

S	M	T	W	T	F	S
		1	2	3	4	5
6	7	8	9	10	11	12
13	14	15	16	17	18	19
20	21	22	23	24	25	26
27	28	29	30			

AUGUST

S	M	T	W	T	F	S
1	2	3	4	5	6	7
8	9	10	11	12	13	14
15	16	17	18	19	20	21
22	23	24	25	26	27	28
29	30	31				

28 | MONDAY

29 | TUESDAY

30 | WEDNESDAY

1 | THURSDAY — Canada Day

2 | FRIDAY

3 | SATURDAY

4 | SUNDAY — Independence Day

Notes

Adult

flight of Steller's and Blue Jays steady
on rowing wingbeats; wingbeats
almost entirely below horizontal

Adult Pacific

Steller's Jay
Cyanocitta stelleri

Overall dark color with paler blue rump
distinctive; shorter-tailed than scrub-jays.
Noisy and conspicuous residents of woods,
often traveling in small groups.

Length 11.5"
Wingspan 19"
Weight 3.7 oz (105 g)

Key to Range Maps

WINTER
SUMMER
YEAR-ROUND
MIGRATION
RARE

July

JUNE

S	M	T	W	T	F	S
		1	2	3	4	5
6	7	8	9	10	11	12
13	14	15	16	17	18	19
20	21	22	23	24	25	26
27	28	29	30			

AUGUST

S	M	T	W	T	F	S
1	2	3	4	5	6	7
8	9	10	11	12	13	14
15	16	17	18	19	20	21
22	23	24	25	26	27	28
29	30	31				

5 | MONDAY

6 | TUESDAY

7 | WEDNESDAY

8 | THURSDAY

9 | FRIDAY

10 | SATURDAY

11 | SUNDAY ⬤ NEW MOON

Notes

Adult

Adult Southern

larger-billed;
darker around eye

Adult Northern

American Magpie
Pica hudsonia

Fairly large and heavy with long tail,
stout bill, broad wings. Formerly
known as Black-billed Magpie.

Length 19"
Wingspan 25"
Weight 6 oz (175 g)
   male > female

Key to Range Maps

WINTER
SUMMER
YEAR-ROUND
MIGRATION
RARE

July

JUNE

S	M	T	W	T	F	S
		1	2	3	4	5
6	7	8	9	10	11	12
13	14	15	16	17	18	19
20	21	22	23	24	25	26
27	28	29	30			

AUGUST

S	M	T	W	T	F	S
1	2	3	4	5	6	7
8	9	10	11	12	13	14
15	16	17	18	19	20	21
22	23	24	25	26	27	28
29	30	31				

12 | MONDAY

13 | TUESDAY

14 | WEDNESDAY

15 | THURSDAY

16 | FRIDAY

17 | SATURDAY

18 | SUNDAY

Notes

Adult male

Adult male
Northeast

Horned Lark
Eremophila alpestris

Fairly slender and long-winged, with
short, stout bill and square tail. Note
dark mask and dark breastband in all
plumages. Flight buoyant and flowing.

Length 7.25"
Wingspan 12"
Weight 1.1 oz (32 g)

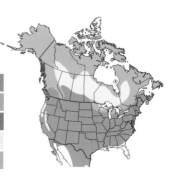

Key to Range Maps

WINTER

SUMMER

YEAR-ROUND

MIGRATION

RARE

July

JUNE

S	M	T	W	T	F	S
		1	2	3	4	5
6	7	8	9	10	11	12
13	14	15	16	17	18	19
20	21	22	23	24	25	26
27	28	29	30			

AUGUST

S	M	T	W	T	F	S
1	2	3	4	5	6	7
8	9	10	11	12	13	14
15	16	17	18	19	20	21
22	23	24	25	26	27	28
29	30	31				

19 | MONDAY

20 | TUESDAY

21 | WEDNESDAY

22 | THURSDAY

23 | FRIDAY

24 | SATURDAY

25 | SUNDAY ○ FULL MOON

Notes

August 2010

MONTH OVERVIEW

JULY
S M T W T F S
            1 2 3
4 5 6 7 8 9 10
11 12 13 14 15 16 17
18 19 20 21 22 23 24
25 26 27 28 29 30 31

SEPTEMBER
S M T W T F S
         1 2 3 4
5 6 7 8 9 10 11
12 13 14 15 16 17 18
19 20 21 22 23 24 25
26 27 28 29 30

SUNDAY	MONDAY	TUESDAY	WEDNESDAY	THURSDAY	FRIDAY	SATURDAY
1	2 Civic Holiday (Canada) Bank Holiday (Canberra, NSW)	3	4	5	6	7
8	9 ● NEW MOON	10	11	12	13	14
15	16	17	18	19	20	21
22	23	24 ○ FULL MOON	25	26	27	28
29	30 Bank Holiday (UK)	31	1	2	3	4

Notes

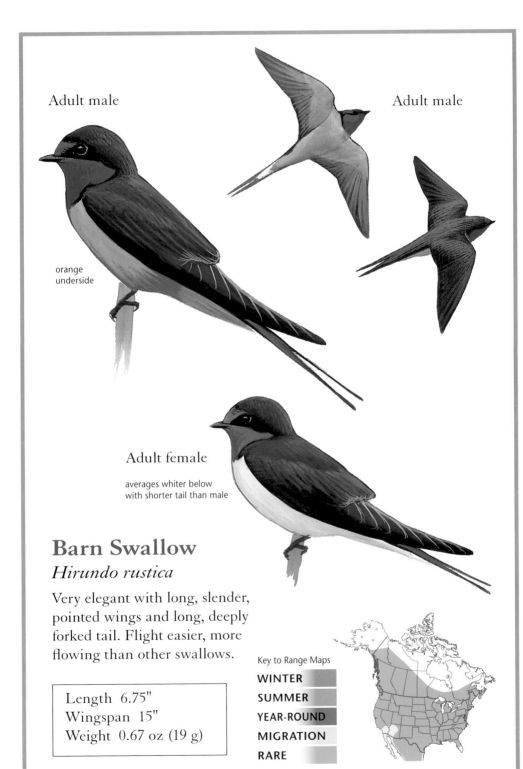

Adult male

Adult male

orange
underside

Adult female

averages whiter below
with shorter tail than male

Barn Swallow
Hirundo rustica

Very elegant with long, slender,
pointed wings and long, deeply
forked tail. Flight easier, more
flowing than other swallows.

Length 6.75"
Wingspan 15"
Weight 0.67 oz (19 g)

Key to Range Maps

WINTER
SUMMER
YEAR-ROUND
MIGRATION
RARE

July/August

JULY

S	M	T	W	T	F	S
				1	2	3
4	5	6	7	8	9	10
11	12	13	14	15	16	17
18	19	20	21	22	23	24
25	26	27	28	29	30	31

SEPTEMBER

S	M	T	W	T	F	S
			1	2	3	4
5	6	7	8	9	10	11
12	13	14	15	16	17	18
19	20	21	22	23	24	25
26	27	28	29	30		

26 | MONDAY

27 | TUESDAY

28 | WEDNESDAY

29 | THURSDAY

30 | FRIDAY

31 | SATURDAY

1 | SUNDAY

Notes

Black-Crested
(Mexican) adult

black crest often raised
higher than Northern

pale
forehead

Black-Crested
(Mexican) adult

Tufted Titmouse
Baeolophus bicolor

Larger than other titmice; larger
and stockier than chickadees. Plain
head, short crest, and relatively
short, broad tail.

Length 6.5"
Wingspan 9.75"
Weight 0.75 oz (21.5 g)

Key to Range Maps

WINTER
SUMMER
YEAR-ROUND
MIGRATION
RARE

August

JULY

S	M	T	W	T	F	S
				1	2	3
4	5	6	7	8	9	10
11	12	13	14	15	16	17
18	19	20	21	22	23	24
25	26	27	28	29	30	31

SEPTEMBER

S	M	T	W	T	F	S
			1	2	3	4
5	6	7	8	9	10	11
12	13	14	15	16	17	18
19	20	21	22	23	24	25
26	27	28	29	30		

2 | MONDAY

Civic Holiday
(Canada)

Bank Holiday
(Canberra, NSW)

3 | TUESDAY

4 | WEDNESDAY

5 | THURSDAY

6 | FRIDAY

7 | SATURDAY

8 | SUNDAY

Notes

Adult

Adult Northern

Carolina Wren
Thryothorus ludovicianus

Large-headed, short-billed, and
stocky overall with bright reddish-
brown plumage.

Length 5.5"
Wingspan 7.5"
Weight 0.74 oz (21 g)

Key to Range Maps

WINTER
SUMMER
YEAR-ROUND
MIGRATION
RARE

August

JULY

S	M	T	W	T	F	S
				1	2	3
4	5	6	7	8	9	10
11	12	13	14	15	16	17
18	19	20	21	22	23	24
25	26	27	28	29	30	31

SEPTEMBER

S	M	T	W	T	F	S
			1	2	3	4
5	6	7	8	9	10	11
12	13	14	15	16	17	18
19	20	21	22	23	24	25
26	27	28	29	30		

9 | MONDAY   ● NEW MOON

10 | TUESDAY

11 | WEDNESDAY

12 | THURSDAY

Notes

13 | FRIDAY

14 | SATURDAY

15 | SUNDAY

Eastern
adult female

Eastern
1st year
female

bright blue-gray

Eastern adult
male breeding
(Mar–Jul)

Blue-gray Gnatcatcher
Polioptila caerulea

Most widespread, often found high in
trees or taller brush. Tiny and long-
tailed, with fairly long, pale bill and
more pointed wings than other
gnatcatchers.

Length 4.5"
Wingspan 6"
Weight 0.21 oz (6 g)

Key to Range Maps

WINTER
SUMMER
YEAR-ROUND
MIGRATION
RARE

August

JULY

S	M	T	W	T	F	S
				1	2	3
4	5	6	7	8	9	10
11	12	13	14	15	16	17
18	19	20	21	22	23	24
25	26	27	28	29	30	31

SEPTEMBER

S	M	T	W	T	F	S
			1	2	3	4
5	6	7	8	9	10	11
12	13	14	15	16	17	18
19	20	21	22	23	24	25
26	27	28	29	30		

16 | MONDAY

17 | TUESDAY

Notes

18 | WEDNESDAY

19 | THURSDAY

20 | FRIDAY

21 | SATURDAY

22 | SUNDAY

Adult male

Adult male

Eastern Bluebird
Sialia sialis

Found in small groups in fields or open woods, often perched on wires or fences. Like Western but smaller overall and slightly thicker-billed.

Length 7"
Wingspan 13"
Weight 1.1 oz (31 g)

Key to Range Maps
WINTER
SUMMER
YEAR-ROUND
MIGRATION
RARE

August

JULY

S	M	T	W	T	F	S
				1	2	3
4	5	6	7	8	9	10
11	12	13	14	15	16	17
18	19	20	21	22	23	24
25	26	27	28	29	30	31

SEPTEMBER

S	M	T	W	T	F	S
			1	2	3	4
5	6	7	8	9	10	11
12	13	14	15	16	17	18
19	20	21	22	23	24	25
26	27	28	29	30		

23 | MONDAY

24 | TUESDAY ○ FULL MOON

25 | WEDNESDAY

26 | THURSDAY

27 | FRIDAY

28 | SATURDAY

29 | SUNDAY

Notes

WEEK 35

September 2010

MONTH OVERVIEW

AUGUST
S M T W T F S
1 2 3 4 5 6 7
8 9 10 11 12 13 14
15 16 17 18 19 20 21
22 23 24 25 26 27 28
29 30 31

OCTOBER
S M T W T F S
1 2
3 4 5 6 7 8 9
10 11 12 13 14 15 16
17 18 19 20 21 22 23
24 25 26 27 28 29 30
31

Sunday	Monday	Tuesday	Wednesday	Thursday	Friday	Saturday
29	30	31	1	2	3	4
5	6 Labor Day (US, Canada)	7	8 ● New Moon	9 Rosh Hashanah	10	11
12	13	14	15	16	17	18 Yom Kippur
19	20	21 UN International Day of Peace	22 Autumnal Equinox	23 ○ Full Moon	24	25
26	27 Queen's Birthday (W. Australia)	28	29	30	1	2

Notes

Adult

jerks wings up over
back to scare insects
out of hiding

Adult

Northern Mockingbird
Mimus polyglottos

Found in open areas near dense
bushes, often in suburban neighbor-
hoods. Northern is aggressive and
conspicuous. Slender-bodied with
long tail and legs; flashing white
wing and tail pattern distinctive.

Length 10"
Wingspan 14"
Weight 1.7 oz (49 g)

Key to Range Maps
WINTER
SUMMER
YEAR-ROUND
MIGRATION
RARE

August/September

AUGUST

S	M	T	W	T	F	S
1	2	3	4	5	6	7
8	9	10	11	12	13	14
15	16	17	18	19	20	21
22	23	24	25	26	27	28
29	30	31				

30 | MONDAY   Bank Holiday (UK)

31 | TUESDAY

OCTOBER

S	M	T	W	T	F	S
					1	2
3	4	5	6	7	8	9
10	11	12	13	14	15	16
17	18	19	20	21	22	23
24	25	26	27	28	29	30
31						

Notes

1 | WEDNESDAY

2 | THURSDAY

3 | FRIDAY

4 | SATURDAY

5 | SUNDAY

Adult

Adult breeding
(Dec-Aug)

walks with waddling gait;
uses bill to pry open grass

European Starling
Sturnus vulgaris

Short, square tail; pointed, triangular
wings; straight, pointed bill. In flight
can be confused with waxwings,
meadowlarks, or Purple Martin.

Length 8.5"
Wingspan 16"
Weight 2.9 oz (82 g)
male > female

Key to Range Maps
WINTER
SUMMER
YEAR-ROUND
MIGRATION
RARE

September

AUGUST

S	M	T	W	T	F	S
1	2	3	4	5	6	7
8	9	10	11	12	13	14
15	16	17	18	19	20	21
22	23	24	25	26	27	28
29	30	31				

OCTOBER

S	M	T	W	T	F	S
					1	2
3	4	5	6	7	8	9
10	11	12	13	14	15	16
17	18	19	20	21	22	23
24	25	26	27	28	29	30
31						

6 MONDAY   Labor Day (US, Canada)

7 TUESDAY

8 WEDNESDAY   ● NEW MOON

9 THURSDAY   Rosh Hashanah

10 FRIDAY

11 SATURDAY

12 SUNDAY

Notes

Darker adult

Darker adult
breeding
(Mar–Jul)

American Pipit
Anthus rubescens

Found on open ground (tundra, beaches, fields), often in flocks. Longer-tailed than other pipits; faintly streaked back and dark legs distinctive.

Length 6.5"
Wingspan 10.5"
Weight 0.74 oz (21 g)

Key to Range Maps

WINTER
SUMMER
YEAR-ROUND
MIGRATION
RARE

September

AUGUST

S	M	T	W	T	F	S
1	2	3	4	5	6	7
8	9	10	11	12	13	14
15	16	17	18	19	20	21
22	23	24	25	26	27	28
29	30	31				

OCTOBER

S	M	T	W	T	F	S
					1	2
3	4	5	6	7	8	9
10	11	12	13	14	15	16
17	18	19	20	21	22	23
24	25	26	27	28	29	30
31						

13 | MONDAY

14 | TUESDAY

15 | WEDNESDAY

16 | THURSDAY

17 | FRIDAY

18 | SATURDAY   Yom Kippur

19 | SUNDAY

Notes

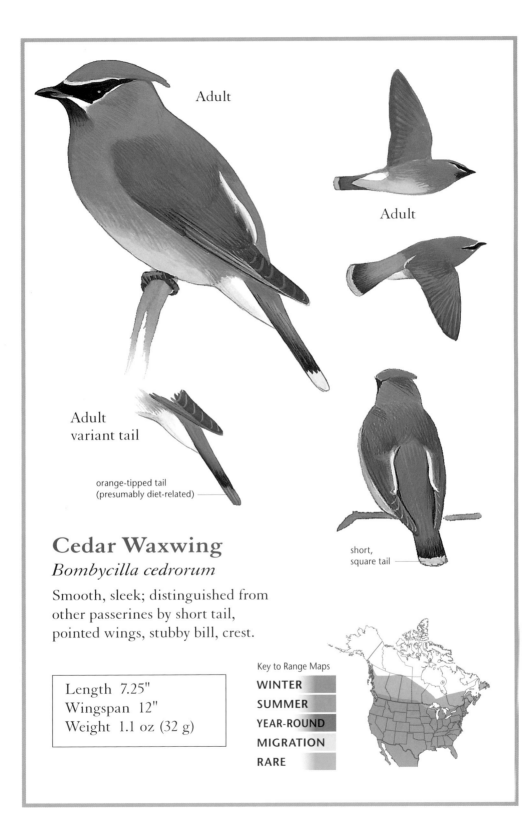

Adult

Adult

Adult
variant tail

orange-tipped tail
(presumably diet-related)

short,
square tail

Cedar Waxwing
Bombycilla cedrorum

Smooth, sleek; distinguished from
other passerines by short tail,
pointed wings, stubby bill, crest.

Length 7.25"
Wingspan 12"
Weight 1.1 oz (32 g)

Key to Range Maps

WINTER

SUMMER

YEAR-ROUND

MIGRATION

RARE

September

AUGUST

S	M	T	W	T	F	S
1	2	3	4	5	6	7
8	9	10	11	12	13	14
15	16	17	18	19	20	21
22	23	24	25	26	27	28
29	30	31				

OCTOBER

S	M	T	W	T	F	S
					1	2
3	4	5	6	7	8	9
10	11	12	13	14	15	16
17	18	19	20	21	22	23
24	25	26	27	28	29	30
31						

20 | MONDAY

21 | TUESDAY   UN International Day of Peace

22 | WEDNESDAY   Autumnal Equinox

23 | THURSDAY   ○ FULL MOON

24 | FRIDAY

25 | SATURDAY

26 | SUNDAY

Notes

October 2010

MONTH OVERVIEW

SEPTEMBER
S	M	T	W	T	F	S
			1	2	3	4
5	6	7	8	9	10	11
12	13	14	15	16	17	18
19	20	21	22	23	24	25
26	27	28	29	30		

NOVEMBER
S	M	T	W	T	F	S
	1	2	3	4	5	6
7	8	9	10	11	12	13
14	15	16	17	18	19	20
21	22	23	24	25	26	27
28	29	30				

SUNDAY	MONDAY	TUESDAY	WEDNESDAY	THURSDAY	FRIDAY	SATURDAY
26	27	28	29	30	1	2
3	4 Labour Day (Canberra, NSW, S. Austrl.)	5	6	7 ● NEW MOON	8	9
10	11 Columbus Day (observed) Thanksgiving (Canada)	12	13	14	15	16
17	18	19	20	21	22 ○ FULL MOON	23
24/31 Halloween (31st)	25 Labour Day (New Zealand)	26	27	28	29	30

Notes

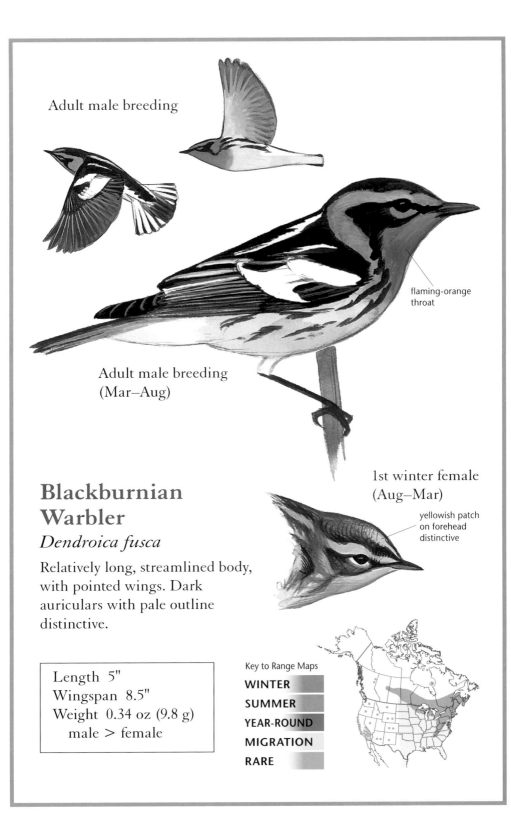

Adult male breeding

Adult male breeding
(Mar–Aug)

flaming-orange
throat

Blackburnian
Warbler
Dendroica fusca

Relatively long, streamlined body,
with pointed wings. Dark
auriculars with pale outline
distinctive.

1st winter female
(Aug–Mar)

yellowish patch
on forehead
distinctive

Length 5"
Wingspan 8.5"
Weight 0.34 oz (9.8 g)
  male > female

Key to Range Maps

WINTER
SUMMER
YEAR-ROUND
MIGRATION
RARE

September/October

SEPTEMBER

S	M	T	W	T	F	S
			1	2	3	4
5	6	7	8	9	10	11
12	13	14	15	16	17	18
19	20	21	22	23	24	25
26	27	28	29	30		

NOVEMBER

S	M	T	W	T	F	S
	1	2	3	4	5	6
7	8	9	10	11	12	13
14	15	16	17	18	19	20
21	22	23	24	25	26	27
28	29	30				

27 | MONDAY — Queen's Birthday (W. Australia)

28 | TUESDAY

29 | WEDNESDAY

30 | THURSDAY

1 | FRIDAY

2 | SATURDAY

3 | SUNDAY

Notes

WEEK 40

Audubon's adult male breeding

Audubon's adult male breeding
(Apr-Aug)

Yellow-rumped Warbler
Dendroica coronata

Rather large; long tail flared at tip;
round head and stout black bill.
Adult male grayish, but all other
plumages washed with brown.

Length 5.5"
Wingspan 9.25"
Weight 0.43 oz (12.3 g)

Key to Range Maps

WINTER
SUMMER
YEAR-ROUND
MIGRATION
RARE

October

SEPTEMBER

S	M	T	W	T	F	S
			1	2	3	4
5	6	7	8	9	10	11
12	13	14	15	16	17	18
19	20	21	22	23	24	25
26	27	28	29	30		

NOVEMBER

S	M	T	W	T	F	S
	1	2	3	4	5	6
7	8	9	10	11	12	13
14	15	16	17	18	19	20
21	22	23	24	25	26	27
28	29	30				

4 | MONDAY — Labour Day
(Canberra, NSW, S. Austrl.)

5 | TUESDAY

6 | WEDNESDAY

7 | THURSDAY — ● NEW MOON

8 | FRIDAY

9 | SATURDAY

10 | SUNDAY

Notes

Adult male
Interior West

Adult

Adult female
Interior West

Common Yellowthroat
Geothlypis trichas

Small and dumpy; short neck, small bill,
round wings, rounded tail. Always shows
contrast between dark malar and
pale throat.

Length 5"
Wingspan 6.75"
Weight 0.35 oz (10 g)

Key to Range Maps

WINTER
SUMMER
YEAR-ROUND
MIGRATION
RARE

October

SEPTEMBER

S	M	T	W	T	F	S
		1	2	3	4
5	6	7	8	9	10	11
12	13	14	15	16	17	18
19	20	21	22	23	24	25
26	27	28	29	30		

11 | MONDAY

Columbus Day
(observed)

Thanksgiving
(Canada)

NOVEMBER

S	M	T	W	T	F	S
	1	2	3	4	5	6
7	8	9	10	11	12	13
14	15	16	17	18	19	20
21	22	23	24	25	26	27
28	29	30				

12 | TUESDAY

13 | WEDNESDAY

Notes

14 | THURSDAY

15 | FRIDAY

16 | SATURDAY

17 | SUNDAY

Adult male

Adult male

rufous
wing-bars

uniform dark blue;
paler on rump

Blue Grosbeak
Guiraca caerulea

Found in brushy or weedy areas
with scattered trees; relatively large-
headed, with heavy bill and
long, rounded tail.

Length 6.75"
Wingspan 11"
Weight 0.98 oz (28 g)

Key to Range Maps

WINTER
SUMMER
YEAR-ROUND
MIGRATION
RARE

October

SEPTEMBER

S	M	T	W	T	F	S
			1	2	3	4
5	6	7	8	9	10	11
12	13	14	15	16	17	18
19	20	21	22	23	24	25
26	27	28	29	30		

NOVEMBER

S	M	T	W	T	F	S
	1	2	3	4	5	6
7	8	9	10	11	12	13
14	15	16	17	18	19	20
21	22	23	24	25	26	27
28	29	30				

18 | MONDAY

19 | TUESDAY

20 | WEDNESDAY

21 | THURSDAY

22 | FRIDAY   ◯ FULL MOON

23 | SATURDAY

24 | SUNDAY

Notes

Adult male

Adult male
breeding
(Apr-Sep)

Adult female
breeding
(Apr-Sep)

Indigo Bunting
Passerina cyanea

Rather stocky, short-tailed, and small-
billed; female best distinguished by
streaked breast and whitish throat.

Length 5.5"
Wingspan 8"
Weight 0.51 oz (14.5 g)

Key to Range Maps

WINTER
SUMMER
YEAR-ROUND
MIGRATION
RARE

October

SEPTEMBER

S	M	T	W	T	F	S
			1	2	3	4
5	6	7	8	9	10	11
12	13	14	15	16	17	18
19	20	21	22	23	24	25
26	27	28	29	30		

NOVEMBER

S	M	T	W	T	F	S
	1	2	3	4	5	6
7	8	9	10	11	12	13
14	15	16	17	18	19	20
21	22	23	24	25	26	27
28	29	30				

25 | MONDAY   Labour Day (New Zealand)

26 | TUESDAY

27 | WEDNESDAY

28 | THURSDAY

29 | FRIDAY

30 | SATURDAY

31 | SUNDAY   Halloween

Notes

WEEK 44

November 2010

MONTH OVERVIEW

OCTOBER

S	M	T	W	T	F	S
					1	2
3	4	5	6	7	8	9
10	11	12	13	14	15	16
17	18	19	20	21	22	23
24	25	26	27	28	29	30
31						

DECEMBER

S	M	T	W	T	F	S
			1	2	3	4
5	6	7	8	9	10	11
12	13	14	15	16	17	18
19	20	21	22	23	24	25
26	27	28	29	30	31	

SUNDAY	MONDAY	TUESDAY	WEDNESDAY	THURSDAY	FRIDAY	SATURDAY
31	1 All Saints' Day	2 Election Day	3	4	5 ● New Moon	6
7 Daylight Saving ends	8	9	10	11 Veterans Day Remembrance Day (Can., Austrl., NZ)	12	13
14 Remembrance Sunday (UK)	15	16	17	18	19	20
21 ○ Full Moon	22	23	24	25 Thanksgiving	26	27
28	29	30	1	2	3	4

Notes

Adult male Red-eyed

Adult male White-eyed

Eastern Towhee
Pipilo erythrophthalmus

Found in dense brush, where they scratch noisily through dead leaves but are often difficult to see. The only towhee over most of its range; larger and stockier than sparrows, with long tail.

Length 8.5"
Wingspan 10.5"
Weight 1.4 oz (40 g)

Key to Range Maps

WINTER
SUMMER
YEAR-ROUND
MIGRATION
RARE

November

OCTOBER

S	M	T	W	T	F	S
					1	2
3	4	5	6	7	8	9
10	11	12	13	14	15	16
17	18	19	20	21	22	23
24	25	26	27	28	29	30
31						

DECEMBER

S	M	T	W	T	F	S
			1	2	3	4
5	6	7	8	9	10	11
12	13	14	15	16	17	18
19	20	21	22	23	24	25
26	27	28	29	30	31	

1 | MONDAY — All Saints' Day

2 | TUESDAY — Election Day

3 | WEDNESDAY

4 | THURSDAY

5 | FRIDAY — ● NEW MOON

6 | SATURDAY

7 | SUNDAY — Daylight Saving ends

Notes

Adult

Adult
Gulf Coast

Adult
Gulf Coast

Seaside Sparrow
Ammodramus maritimus

Found exclusively in saltmarsh grass,
distinguished from other sparrows by
its large size, overall dark gray color,
white throat, and long bill.

Length 6"
Wingspan 7.5"
Weight 0.81 oz (23 g)

Key to Range Maps

WINTER
SUMMER
YEAR-ROUND
MIGRATION
RARE

November

OCTOBER
S	M	T	W	T	F	S
					1	2
3	4	5	6	7	8	9
10	11	12	13	14	15	16
17	18	19	20	21	22	23
24	25	26	27	28	29	30
31						

DECEMBER
S	M	T	W	T	F	S
			1	2	3	4
5	6	7	8	9	10	11
12	13	14	15	16	17	18
19	20	21	22	23	24	25
26	27	28	29	30	31	

8 | MONDAY

9 | TUESDAY

10 | WEDNESDAY

11 | THURSDAY
Veterans Day
Remembrance Day
(Can., Austrl., NZ)

12 | FRIDAY

13 | SATURDAY

14 | SUNDAY
Remembrance Sunday (UK)

Notes

Adult male
breeding

all-black

Adult male
breeding
(Mar-Jul)

Lark Bunting
Calamospiza melanocorys

Found in arid, grassy or brushy areas,
often in very large flocks in winter.
Large and stocky; broad-headed,
large-billed, with short tail and
short, rounded wings.

Length 7"
Wingspan 10.5"
Weight 1.3 oz (38 g)

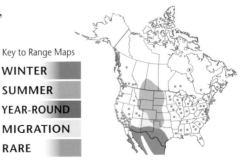

Key to Range Maps

WINTER
SUMMER
YEAR-ROUND
MIGRATION
RARE

November

OCTOBER

S	M	T	W	T	F	S
					1	2
3	4	5	6	7	8	9
10	11	12	13	14	15	16
17	18	19	20	21	22	23
24	25	26	27	28	29	30
31						

DECEMBER

S	M	T	W	T	F	S
			1	2	3	4
5	6	7	8	9	10	11
12	13	14	15	16	17	18
19	20	21	22	23	24	25
26	27	28	29	30	31	

15 | MONDAY

16 | TUESDAY

17 | WEDNESDAY

18 | THURSDAY

19 | FRIDAY

20 | SATURDAY

21 | SUNDAY

○ FULL MOON

Notes

White-winged
adult

White-winged
adult male

Dark-eyed Junco
Junco hyemalis

The largest junco; averages 12 percent
larger than other juncos, with relatively
larger bill. Rather pale gray overall
(palest on throat), with weak wing-bars
and extensive white on tail.

White-winged
1st year female

Length 6.25"
Wingspan 9.25"
Weight 0.67 oz (19 g)

Key to Range Maps

WINTER
SUMMER
YEAR-ROUND
MIGRATION
RARE

November

OCTOBER

S	M	T	W	T	F	S
					1	2
3	4	5	6	7	8	9
10	11	12	13	14	15	16
17	18	19	20	21	22	23
24	25	26	27	28	29	30
31						

DECEMBER

S	M	T	W	T	F	S
			1	2	3	4
5	6	7	8	9	10	11
12	13	14	15	16	17	18
19	20	21	22	23	24	25
26	27	28	29	30	31	

22 | MONDAY

23 | TUESDAY

Notes

24 | WEDNESDAY

25 | THURSDAY   Thanksgiving

26 | FRIDAY

27 | SATURDAY

28 | SUNDAY

December 2010

MONTH OVERVIEW

NOVEMBER
S M T W T F S
1 2 3 4 5 6
7 8 9 10 11 12 13
14 15 16 17 18 19 20
21 22 23 24 25 26 27
28 29 30

JANUARY 2011
S M T W T F S
1
2 3 4 5 6 7 8
9 10 11 12 13 14 15
16 17 18 19 20 21 22
23 24 25 26 27 28 29
30 31

SUNDAY	MONDAY	TUESDAY	WEDNESDAY	THURSDAY	FRIDAY	SATURDAY
28	29	30	1	2 Hanukkah begins	3	4
5 ● New Moon	6	7 Pearl Harbor Day	8	9	10	11
12	13	14	15	16	17	18
19	20	21 Winter Solstice ○ Full Moon	22	23	24	25 Christmas
26 Boxing Day (Can., UK, Austrl., NZ) Kwanzaa begins	27 Bank Holiday (UK, Austrl., NZ)	28 Bank Holiday (UK, Austrl., NZ)	29	30	31	1

Notes

Adult male

Adult male breeding
(Mar–Aug)

Snow Bunting
Plectrophenax nivalis

Found in flocks on barren, open ground
— beaches, fields, tundra. Larger than
longspurs and Horned Larks with fluffy
plumage, shuffling gait, and flashing
white wing-patches.

Length 6.75"
Wingspan 14"
Weight 1.5 oz (42 g)

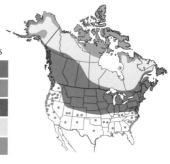

Key to Range Maps

WINTER
SUMMER
YEAR-ROUND
MIGRATION
RARE

November/December

NOVEMBER

S	M	T	W	T	F	S
	1	2	3	4	5	6
7	8	9	10	11	12	13
14	15	16	17	18	19	20
21	22	23	24	25	26	27
28	29	30				

JANUARY 2011

S	M	T	W	T	F	S
						1
2	3	4	5	6	7	8
9	10	11	12	13	14	15
16	17	18	19	20	21	22
23	24	25	26	27	28	29
30	31					

29 | MONDAY

30 | TUESDAY

1 | WEDNESDAY

2 | THURSDAY   Hanukkah begins

3 | FRIDAY

4 | SATURDAY

5 | SUNDAY   ● NEW MOON

Notes

Typical adult breeding
(Feb-Aug)

mostly
white malar

streaks

Typical adult

contrasting dark
head-stripes

Typical adult
nonbreeding
(Sep-Jan)

rufous overall

Eastern
Meadowlark
Sturnella magna

Found in open, grassy habitats, often
perching on fences or bushes in small,
loose flocks. Plumage characteristics
very subtle.

Length 9.5"
Wingspan 14"
Weight 3.2 oz (90 g)
   male > female

Key to Range Maps

WINTER
SUMMER
YEAR-ROUND
MIGRATION
RARE

December

NOVEMBER

S	M	T	W	T	F	S
	1	2	3	4	5	6
7	8	9	10	11	12	13
14	15	16	17	18	19	20
21	22	23	24	25	26	27
28	29	30				

JANUARY 2011

S	M	T	W	T	F	S
						1
2	3	4	5	6	7	8
9	10	11	12	13	14	15
16	17	18	19	20	21	22
23	24	25	26	27	28	29
30	31					

6 MONDAY

7 TUESDAY — Pearl Harbor Day

8 WEDNESDAY

9 THURSDAY

10 FRIDAY

11 SATURDAY

12 SUNDAY

Notes

WEEK 50

Adult male

Adult male

drab brownish sides
of neck and head

Drab 1st year
female

Baltimore Oriole
Icterus galbula

Found in open broadleaf woods,
foraging among leaves in trees.
The brightest color is on the breast.

Length 8.75"
Wingspan 11.5"
Weight 1.2 oz (33 g)

Key to Range Maps

WINTER

SUMMER

YEAR-ROUND

MIGRATION

RARE

December

NOVEMBER

S	M	T	W	T	F	S
	1	2	3	4	5	6
7	8	9	10	11	12	13
14	15	16	17	18	19	20
21	22	23	24	25	26	27
28	29	30				

JANUARY 2011

S	M	T	W	T	F	S
						1
2	3	4	5	6	7	8
9	10	11	12	13	14	15
16	17	18	19	20	21	22
23	24	25	26	27	28	29
30	31					

13 | MONDAY

14 | TUESDAY

15 | WEDNESDAY

16 | THURSDAY

17 | FRIDAY

18 | SATURDAY

19 | SUNDAY

Notes

Adult male

Adult male

Adult male

dull red

Red Crossbill
Loxia curvirostra

Relatively large-headed and short-tailed, with
long, pointed wings; bill varies in size but
generally large. Clambers parrotlike over
pinecones, using short legs
and stout bill.

Length 6.25"
Wingspan 11"
Weight 1.3 oz (36 g)

Key to Range Maps

WINTER
SUMMER
YEAR-ROUND
MIGRATION
RARE

December

NOVEMBER

S	M	T	W	T	F	S
	1	2	3	4	5	6
7	8	9	10	11	12	13
14	15	16	17	18	19	20
21	22	23	24	25	26	27
28	29	30				

JANUARY 2011

S	M	T	W	T	F	S
						1
2	3	4	5	6	7	8
9	10	11	12	13	14	15
16	17	18	19	20	21	22
23	24	25	26	27	28	29
30	31					

20 | MONDAY

21 | TUESDAY

Winter Solstice
○ FULL MOON

Notes

22 | WEDNESDAY

23 | THURSDAY

24 | FRIDAY

25 | SATURDAY

Christmas

26 | SUNDAY

Boxing Day
(Can., UK, Austrl., NZ)

Kwanzaa begins

WEEK 52

December 2010/
January 2011

DECEMBER

S	M	T	W	T	F	S
			1	2	3	4
5	6	7	8	9	10	11
12	13	14	15	16	17	18
19	20	21	22	23	24	25
26	27	28	29	30	31	

FEBRUARY

S	M	T	W	T	F	S
		1	2	3	4	5
6	7	8	9	10	11	12
13	14	15	16	17	18	19
20	21	22	23	24	25	26
27	28					

27 MONDAY — Bank Holiday (UK, Austrl., NZ)

28 TUESDAY — Bank Holiday (UK, Austrl., NZ)

29 WEDNESDAY

30 THURSDAY

31 FRIDAY

1 SATURDAY — New Year's Day 2011

2 SUNDAY

Notes

2011 Year-At-A-Glance

JANUARY

S	M	T	W	T	F	S
						1
2	3	4	5	6	7	8
9	10	11	12	13	14	15
16	17	18	19	20	21	22
23	24	25	26	27	28	29
30	31					

FEBRUARY

S	M	T	W	T	F	S
		1	2	3	4	5
6	7	8	9	10	11	12
13	14	15	16	17	18	19
20	21	22	23	24	25	26
27	28					

MARCH

S	M	T	W	T	F	S
		1	2	3	4	5
6	7	8	9	10	11	12
13	14	15	16	17	18	19
20	21	22	23	24	25	26
27	28	29	30	31		

APRIL

S	M	T	W	T	F	S
					1	2
3	4	5	6	7	8	9
10	11	12	13	14	15	16
17	18	19	20	21	22	23
24	25	26	27	28	29	30

MAY

S	M	T	W	T	F	S
1	2	3	4	5	6	7
8	9	10	11	12	13	14
15	16	17	18	19	20	21
22	23	24	25	26	27	28
29	30	31				

JUNE

S	M	T	W	T	F	S
			1	2	3	4
5	6	7	8	9	10	11
12	13	14	15	16	17	18
19	20	21	22	23	24	25
26	27	28	29	30		

JULY

S	M	T	W	T	F	S
					1	2
3	4	5	6	7	8	9
10	11	12	13	14	15	16
17	18	19	20	21	22	23
24	25	26	27	28	29	30
31						

AUGUST

S	M	T	W	T	F	S
	1	2	3	4	5	6
7	8	9	10	11	12	13
14	15	16	17	18	19	20
21	22	23	24	25	26	27
28	29	30	31			

SEPTEMBER

S	M	T	W	T	F	S
				1	2	3
4	5	6	7	8	9	10
11	12	13	14	15	16	17
18	19	20	21	22	23	24
25	26	27	28	29	30	

OCTOBER

S	M	T	W	T	F	S
						1
2	3	4	5	6	7	8
9	10	11	12	13	14	15
16	17	18	19	20	21	22
23	24	25	26	27	28	29
30	31					

NOVEMBER

S	M	T	W	T	F	S
		1	2	3	4	5
6	7	8	9	10	11	12
13	14	15	16	17	18	19
20	21	22	23	24	25	26
27	28	29	30			

DECEMBER

S	M	T	W	T	F	S
				1	2	3
4	5	6	7	8	9	10
11	12	13	14	15	16	17
18	19	20	21	22	23	24
25	26	27	28	29	30	31

Important Dates to Remember for 2011

JANUARY 2011

FEBRUARY 2011

MARCH 2011

APRIL 2011

MAY 2011

JUNE 2011

JULY 2011

AUGUST 2011

SEPTEMBER 2011

OCTOBER 2011

NOVEMBER 2011

DECEMBER 2011

Contacts

NAME	CONTACT INFORMATION

Contacts

NAME	CONTACT INFORMATION

Contacts

NAME	CONTACT INFORMATION

CONTACTS

NAME	CONTACT INFORMATION

Notes

Notes

Calendar © 2009 Sellers Publishing, Inc.
Text © 2000 David Sibley
Illustrations © 2000, 2002, 2003, 2009 David Sibley
All rights reserved.

Published by Sellers Publishing, Inc.
161 John Roberts Road, South Portland, Maine 04106
For ordering information:
Phone: (800) MAKE-FUN (625-3386) Fax: (207) 772-6814
Visit our Web site: www.makefun.com E-mail: rsp@rsvp.com
Canadian Stores contact: Jannex (905) 284-8484

ISBN 13: 978-1-4162-8357-7

Printed in China

Jewish holidays begin at sunset on the previous evening.
Astronomical information is in Eastern Standard Time.
Key to abbreviations: United States (US), Canada (Can.), United Kingdom
(UK), Australia (Austrl.), New Zealand (NZ), New South Wales (NSW)
*This calendar may not be reproduced by any means, including photocopying,
without the prior written permission of the publisher.*